The Gardener's Guide to
SUCCULENTS

A Handbook of Over 125 Exquisite Varieties of Succulents and Cacti

Misa Matsuyama

TUTTLE Publishing

Tokyo | Rutland, Vermont | Singapore

CONTENTS

PART 1 The Varieties of Succulent Plants

A key to care and requirements

Ventilation
★ Be careful in extreme summer conditions
★★★ Be very careful year-round

Cold
★ Tolerates some cold
★★★ Very vulnerable to cold. Keep indoors in fall (depending on region) and winter.

Light intensity
★ Avoid very strong sunlight
★★★ Direct summer sunlight can cause leaf burn.

Light shortage
★ Can tolerate low sunlight
★★★ Lack of sunlight can cause discoloration and spindly growth

Growth rate:
★ Slow ★★ Average ★★★ Fast

★ These stars provide general information on a plant's requirements and issues, and are for reference only. Your plant's needs will vary depending on the plant's condition, the soil and so on.

PART 3 | Creating Succulent Arrangements

Introduction

Succulent plants originated in areas that receive extremely low rainfall. Because of this, they evolved in a way that would enable them to accumulate water inside their bodies. The shapes born from such strength are beautiful and strange.

Unlike other plants, their leaves have very delicate color gradients. The leaves also change color during fall and are truly a wonderful sight.

I hope that with the help of this illustrated book, you'll enjoy discovering these wonderful plants and become acquainted with their details almost as if you were observing them through a magnifying glass. I think the best way to appreciate the beauty of succulent plants is by looking up close, and learning as much as you can about their origins and characteristics.

There are many types of succulents, and it's fun to collect them. Most of the species I introduce in this book are among the more accessible types, and should be fairly easy to come by. I hope this book will entice you to give succulents a try, and maybe set you on the road to a new passion.

— Misa Matsuyama

PART 1

The Varieties of Succulent Plants

In this section, I will introduce the species' main characteristics—how they look, how they grow, and other aspects—in order to give you a sense of their infinite variety. For example, *Sedum* plants have plump leaves filled entirely with water, while *Haworthia* and others have a "lens" that gleams and which, if seen from the right angle, is truly beautiful. And the *Lithops* have a skin that they shed.

The world of succulents is vast, mysterious and fascinating. This is the world I hope to share with you. I hope you enjoy the adventure.

Plump leaves In order to protect themselves from dehydration, succulents have thick and plump leaves that are full of water. The ability to retain water is a defining characteristic of succulents and cacti, and leaves such as you see on succulents won't be found on other types of plant.

Sedum
(Stonecrops/
Crassulaceae
Family)

Characteristics: *Sedum* are so named because of the way they spread or creep low to the ground, growing in clumps or clusters. They are popular for rooftop greening, rock gardens, and other places where soil may be shallow. The leaves come in many colors and shapes as well.

Cultivation: *Sedum* grow fast. They can be kept neat by regular trimming. It is important to keep them in a sunny area, as they really love sunlight. Being strong to cold weather, they can be grown outdoors all year round. If grown indoors, they might not receive enough sunlight, making them more difficult to sustain and grow cleanly.

Area of origin: Tropic, subtropic, temperate areas

Ventilation ★★★
Light shortage ★★★
Growth rate ★★

Sedum dasyphyllum (Corsican stonecrop)

This variety is made of small clumps of blue, fuzzy leaves. Its flowers are charming white florets. It can grow into a beautiful carpet or cascade. Be sure to ensure good ventilation, as this plant can rot easily in the summer months. In the fall the leaves change to a beautiful purple. It is easy to breed and it can easily grow outside of summer.

Sedum hernandezii

Ventilation ★★
Light shortage ★★
Growth rate ★

The leaves are deep green in color, with brown, fuzzy stems. Its growth is very slow. Since it easily gets sunburned, avoid strong sunlight in midsummer.

Sedum hernandezii

Sedum pachyphyllum

Sedum spathulifolium
(Broadleaf stonecrop)

Ventilation ★★★
Light shortage ★★★
Growth rate ★★

Stems and leaves are covered in a white powder. It grows small, pretty rose-shaped leaf clusters. It's extremely weak to rotting during summer and requires care. As the plant ages, the distance between the leaves also increases.

Sedum pachyphyllum

Ventilation ★★★
Light shortage ★★★
Growth rate ★★

Called "Maiden's heart" (or also "Maiden's mind" or "Maiden's feelings") in Japanese because the tip of the leaves "blush" during the fall. It's prone to rotting during summer, so make sure it's placed in a very ventilated spot.

Sedum spathulifolium

Sedum 'Rotty'

Ventilation ★★★
Light shortage ★★
Growth rate ★★

This is a hybrid species, popular for its flowers. In the fall, only the edges turn red. The lower leaves wither and fall, growing back like "pup plants."

Sedum 'Rotty'

Ventilation ★★★
Light shortage ★★
Growth rate ★★

Sedum rubrotinctum f. variegata

This plant paints itself a beautiful pink color in the fall and has variegated rainbow spots. If it doesn't receive sufficient sunlight, the pink color will be pale or dull. The color is also affected by the amount of water the plant absorbs; for best results, give only a moderate amount of water.

Sedum rubrotinctum f. variegata

Sedum rubrotinctum

Ventilation ★★★
Light shortage ★★★
Growth rate ★★

Sedum rubrotinctum

Without a doubt this is one of the most representative species of succulents. It has plump red leaves that have earned it the nickname "Jellybean plant." It's green in summer and a strong red in the fall. It grows best if placed in well-lit spaces and given moderate amounts of water. Being strong to both hot and cold weather, it can be grown outdoors all year long. Its bright red color can help accentuate any other plant.

Sedum makinoi f. variegata

Ventilation ★★★
Light shortage ★★★
Growth rate ★★★

With wonderful round leaves, this is a beautiful variegated perennial plant. It grows gradually. It's a popular choice for greening rooftops. If placed under strong sunlight outdoors, it could extend and overgrow.

Sedum makinoi f. variegata

Sedum dendroideum

Sedum dendroideum
(Tree stonecrop)

Ventilation ★★
Light shortage ★★★
Growth rate ★★

This species grows very large and tree-like in shape. In the fall it becomes plump, and the whole stem turns yellow while the leaves turn pink. The lower leaves fall, and only upper leaves that can reach sunlight remain. If planted in a grouping it makes a strong specimen plant.

<table>
<tr><td>

Pachyphytum
(Stonecrops/
Crassulaceae
Family)

</td><td>

Characteristics: It has thick, plump leaves. Its growth is very slow, but if it is kept in good sunlight, it's very beautiful once it's grown. Its pale blue and gray colors change to a shade of pink in the fall.

Cultivation: It's an easy plant to grow, strong to both hot and cold weather. It grows best if put in a well-lit place. However, monitor the plant regularly, as overly strong sunlight might damage the surface of the leaves. Species that have coated leaves are also sensitive to touch, as the oils from human skin can damage their protective coating.

Area of origin: Mexico

</td></tr>
</table>

Pachyphytum oviferum

Light intensity ★★★
Light shortage ★★
Growth rate ★

In the fall it changes to a wonderful pink color. The white powder that covers the surface helps give shading to the plant. It gradually grows many leaves. This plant grows upwards. If paired with a shorter plant, such as *Sedum*, placed beneath it, it creates a lively scene.

Cotyledon (Stonecrops/ Crassulaceae Family)	**Characteristics**: The *Cotyledon* genus has thick leaves and grows in clusters. The lower part is firm and tree-shaped. Its flowers are big, beautiful and bell shaped. **Cultivation**: It easily grows strong, but also grows slowly. It acquires a stunning shape if kept under sunlight and is regularly monitored and tended. The variants that have white powder on their leaves especially love the sunlight. If the surface of the leaves is covered in hair instead, they are vulnerable to summer heat, thus requiring extra care to prevent rot. **Area of origin**: South Africa.

Cotyledon ladismithensis

Cotyledon ladismithensis

Ventilation ★★★
Light shortage ★★
Growth rate ★

Also called "Bear's paw" because of the shape of their leaves. The tips of the leaves are called "nails," and they turn red in the fall. In summer it's vulnerable to rotting, and the number of leaves will temporarily decrease. Keep the watering in summer very moderate. Growth happens mostly during the fall.

Cotyledon tomentosa ssp. ladismithiensis

Ventilation ★★★
Light shortage ★★
Growth rate ★

Its leaves are smaller compared to *Cotyledon ladismithensis* and have only three nails. It is weak to summer heat so let it air out and rest well. As with *Cotyledon ladismithensis*, give only moderate amounts of water during summer.

Cotyledon tomentosa ssp. ladismithiensis

Cotyledon macrantha var. virescens

Cotyledon macrantha var. virescens

This is a large variant with large leaves supported by a thick stem. The leaves are a deep green and only the edges turn red in the fall. The lower leaves tend to wither while the plant grows upwards.

Ventilation ★★
Light shortage ★★
Growth rate ★

Cotyledon undulata

Cotyledon undulata

Ventilation ★★
Light shortage ★★★
Growth rate ★

This plant, also called "Silver crown" and 'Silver ruffles," is coated in a white powder. It really loves being in sunlight and can be kept outdoors all year long. Its flower blooms in a large orange bell shape. When blooming, keep under sunlight and water more than usual.

Cotyledon orbiculata var. oophylla
(Round-leafed navel-wort)

Ventilation ★★
Light shortage ★★★
Growth rate ★

Small variant with puffy, round leaves. The surface is covered in white powder. It looks even nicer in the fall when the leaves' edges become red. The lower leaves tend to wither while the plant grows upwards in a tree-like shape.

Cotyledon orbiculata var. oophylla

Cotyledon cv. 'Tinkerbell'

The beautiful smooth, pale green leaves are the source of its popularity. The thin brown stems become solid wood branches and it can grow to about a foot (30 cm).

Ventilation ★
Light shortage ★★★
Growth rate ★

Cotyledon cv. 'Tinkerbell'

13

Adromischus (Stonecrops/ Crassulaceae Family)	**Characteristics:** It has puffy leaves that can have all kinds of patterns on their surfaces. Its growth is very slow. The stems of some varieties are covered in hair. These plants require extra care when handling, because it's very easy to accidentally remove leaves.

Cultivation: It is very strong. Since the leaves are thick, they can be used for cutting (asexual reproduction).

Area of origin: South Africa.

Adromischus trigynus

Adromischus trigynus

Ventilation ★★★
Growth rate ★

This plant is characterized by leaves with fascinating red and brown patterns. The flowers are very simple but also bloom very easily. It requires care in summer to protect it from rot.

Adromischus cristatus

Adromischus cristatus

Ventilation ★★★
Growth rate ★

The frilly edges of the leaves have earned it the nickname "Crinkle-leaf plant" and the hair-covered stem gives it a kind of mysterious look. Although its growth is very slow, once it grows and stands up it has a very powerful presence. It grows appreciably each year.

Originally from areas with strong sunlight, most of their bodies are covered by sand. The only part that's left exposed are the lens-like leaves, which evolved in order to take in more light.

Haworthia
(Lilies/Liliaceae family)

Characteristics: *Haworthia* (also called *Haorsia*) has a lens on the surface of the leaf in order to collect light. It keeps these leaves as its only window on the outside while the rest of the body is hidden under the sand. The lenses can vary greatly in transparency, and usually the more transparent types are more popular. Patterns on the leaves also vary greatly, which adds to the fun of collecting these plants. The flowers have white, shiny petals and they grow straight from the body, blooming upwards. The flowers themselves may not be gorgeous but the plant has a great overall charm.

Cultivation: It's very similar in nature to *Gasteria*. It can be grown in places with relatively low sunlight, such as window fronts. The more transparent it is, the more it wants sunlight. If the leaves start to turn brown, it means that the sunlight is too strong; if the rosette collapses and the leaves start to stand upright, it means the plant isn't receiving enough sunlight.

Area of origin: South Africa

Haworthia obtusa

Haworthia obtusa

Light shortage　★
Light intensity　★★
Growth rate　★

This is a very popular variety, due to the beautiful transparent lens on the tip of the leaves. Each leaf looks like a drop of water. Once the plant grows to about 4 inches (10 cm) in diameter, it starts growing pups in a cluster. Being very different in nature from other succulent plants, it is easier to manage when grouped with other plants from the *Haworthia* family.

Haworthia correcta

Light shortage　★
Light intensity　★★
Growth rate　★

Various types of patterns and shapes can be seen on the leaves' surface. The lens is large and the veins are unique. If the sunlight it receives is too strong the plant will turn brown. If the sunlight is too weak the plant stretches upward, seeking light, creating gapping between the leaves.

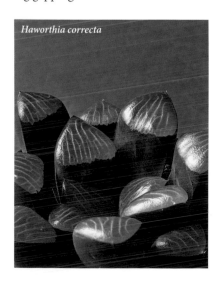

Haworthia correcta

Haworthia reinwardtii

Haworthia reinwardtii

This variety has hard leaves with a white pattern. It is very similar to *Haworthia fasciata* but the leaves expand without spreading. It grows pups in clusters. If the leaves spread out it means that sunlight is lacking.

Light shortage ★★
Light intensity ★★
Growth rate ★

Haworthia arachnoidea v. gigas

Haworthia arachnoidea v. gigas

Light shortage ★★
Light intensity ★★
Growth rate ★

It covers its edges with plastic-like hair and forms a rosette that goes inwards. Growth is slow. In order to avoid sunburn, avoid strong sunlight and do not let it dehydrate, so that it can grow slowly into a relatively large plant.

Haworthia cv. 'Kegani'

Haworthia cv. 'Kegani'

Light intensity ★★★
Growth rate ★

A crossbreed variation. In younger plants, the leaves grow in two fanned-our rows. The fuzzy feel of the leaf is similar to that of a hairbrush. There are also other variations of "crab" *haworthia*. It is very vulnerable to sunburn, so it should be grown out of direct sunlight.

Haworthia truncata

While the leaves may look as if they've been snapped or cut, they really do grow this way, earning this plant the nickname "Horse's teeth." The flat surface on top of the leaves is a lens that collects light. This plant can be extremely expensive depending on the pattern of the lens. It's also very vulnerable to sunburn, so be careful of sunlight in summer.

Haworthia truncata

Light intensity ★★★
Growth rate ★

Fenestraria
(Stone Plants/ Aizoceae family)

Characteristics: The thick leaf surface has a window-like lens that can collect light. That windowed tip is the only part of the plant that pushes past the soil's surface. Flowers can be white or yellow (such as in the case of *Fenestraria aurantiaca*). The color of the flowers is unknown until they bloom and they are mostly similar in appearance.

Cultivation: This is a genus that grows in winter and rests during summer. It is especially vulnerable to summer heat. During summer place it in a well-ventilated, not-too-bright place and do not water it. In winter it's extremely strong against the cold, so it can even be left outdoors. Once it survives the summer, it's mostly easy to grow.

Area of origin: South Africa.

Fenestraria aurantiaca

Ventilation ★★★
Light shortage ★
Growth rate ★

Also known as "Baby toes," this plant has yellow flowers. It opens during daytime and closes in the evening. The leaves are slightly longer compared to other variants of *Fenestraria*. The translucent dome of the leaf tips gives this plant a unique beauty. It's recommended to plant it along with other plants from the *Aizoceae* family.

Conophytum
(Stone Plants/ Aizoceae family)

Characteristics: These oddly-shaped plants are full of charm. There are many variations—so many that it's difficult to distinguish them. It forms a kind of ball with two leaves attached to it. The shape of this ball can vary among round, oval or pocket shapes. In winter it grows flowers that come in red, white, yellow and purple shades, and are so beautiful that some gardeners try to collect each color.

Cultivation: It's a species that grows in winter and rests during summer. It is especially vulnerable to summer heat. During summer let it rest in a well-ventilated spot that's not too bright, and do not water it. In spring it begins to shed its skin (molt) and loses its tension. New pup plants grow from the middle of the plant. If it doesn't receive enough sunlight it grows vertically but is weak, so it's best to grow it in a well-lit spot.

Area of origin: South Africa.

Conophytum igniflorum

Ventilation ★★★
Light shortage ★★
Growth rate ★

Its heart shape and the thick figure are what makes this variant popular. It blooms beautiful orange flowers. From the end of spring to fall keep it in a well-ventilated space and give it barely any water.

Molting

The shedding of skin is animal phenomenon that appears to be very unusual for plants. Molting allows the plant to breed from one individual to two. The next generation grows slowly inside the previous one. Once fully grown, it breaks out.

Lithops
(Stone Plants/
Aizoceae family)

Characteristics: Like *Conophytum*, this particular plant has two leaves arranged in a rounded shape. The pattern on the plant is meant to mimic the stones nearby, providing camouflage against animals. There are numerous variants, and it can grow flowers in a vast array of colors, making it popular among collectors. "Lithops" quite literally means "similar to a stone."

Cultivation: Also like *Conophytum*, *Lithops* grows in winter and rests during summer. It is especially vulnerable to summer heat. During summer let it rest in a well-ventilated not-too-bright place and do not water it. In spring it begins to molt its skin and loses its tension; start reducing the amount of watering once that happens. New pup plants grow and come out from the middle. If sunlight is inadequate the plant grows vertically but weak, so it's best to grow it in a well-lit spot.

Area of origin: South Africa

Ventilation ★★★
Light shortage ★★
Growth rate ★

Lithops aucampiae ssp. aucampiae

The leaves becomes large and the window has a strong impact on the eye. It grows a beautiful yellow flower on the reddish skin. It's very easy to grow along with other plants of the same family. There are many variants of *Lithops* and they are all the same in nature, making it fun to grow them together.

Rosettes look like a blooming flower, with regular overlapping leaves spreading outward. If grouped together they can spread colorfully in the fall like a flower garden.

Echeveria
(Stonecrops/
Crassulaceae
Family)

Characteristics: Its leaves spread like flower petals and it's popular for its beautiful form and appearance. It's also very popular among collectors due to the many color and shape variations this genus has to offer. Pups can either grow sideways or grow from the withered lower leaves.

Cultivation: If you're attentive to ventilation, it's easy to grow an *Echeveria* all year long. It grows more beautiful if grown outdoors rather than indoors. Strong sunlight is required during summer in order to keep the leaves red during winter. It's vulnerable to insects, so it's important to detect bugs early and remove them appropriately.

Area of origin: Mid-south America

Echeveria cv. 'Party Dress'

Echeveria cv. 'Party Dress'

Ventilation ★★★
Light shortage ★★★
Growth rate ★★

Large and beautiful, this plant changes to a deeper pink color in the fall. The leaves are large and sturdy. This variety is strong and easy to grow but requires quite a bit of space when grouped with other plants.

Echeveria chihuahuaensis

Echeveria chihuahuaensis

Ventilation ★★★
Light shortage ★★★
Growth rate ★★

This is a small variant. It's a cute, compact rosette with pink leaves. Since the leaves are pink in color all year long, this plant can be used to add some color to a group planting. Ensure good ventilation, as this plant is very vulnerable to summer heat.

Echeveria cv. 'Topsy Turvy'

Echeveria cv. 'Topsy Turvy'

Ventilation ★★
Light shortage ★★★
Growth rate ★★

Each leaf rises and curls toward the center. The surface of the leaves is covered in pale white powder. In the fall its color changes to a pale pink. The leaves form a sort of heart shape. Despite being slightly vulnerable to rotting, it's easy to grow. It also grows nice flowers. Due to the characteristic shape of its leaves, it stands out when planted in multiples.

Echeveria cv. 'Bombycina'

Echeveria 'Laulindsa'

Ventilation ★★★
Light shortage ★★★
Growth rate ★★

A rosette with thick leaves covered in pale bluish-white powder. It's weak to summer rotting so keep it well-ventilated. The leaves are plump from fall to spring, and in the fall they take on a beautiful pink color. Since it's very weak to heat, it's better to not plant it near other plants.

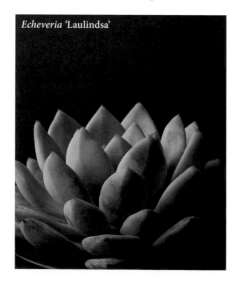
Echeveria 'Laulindsa'

Echeveria cv. 'Bombycina'

Ventilation ★★★
Light shortage ★★★
Growth rate ★★

Fluffy, hairy leaves and stems make this plant look almost like a pet. It's especially vulnerable to heat and rotting in summer, so be sure to place it in a in a well-ventilated spot. The lower leaves wither and grow into new plants. Because of its vulnerability to heat, it's better to avoid planting them too closely together so as to provide them with the ventilation they need.

Echeveria harmsii

Echeveria 'Iria' f. cristata

Echeveria harmsii

Ventilation ★★
Light shortage ★★★
Growth rate ★★

In the fall, this plant turns red in the center. It grows in a lovely tree shape. The leaves are long during growth periods, and become shorter and compact during the fall. Its appearance changes along with seasons. It works well in the lead role in a group planting.

Echeveria 'Iria' f. cristata

It has a beautiful form with overlapping leaves that look like thin lace. The overlapping gives this plant particular beauty and fullness. In the fall it changes from pale blue to pale green. Compared to other *Echeveria* it requires more ventilation during summer.

Echeveria 'Gusto'

Echeveria 'Gusto'

Ventilation ★★
Light shortage ★★
Growth rate ★★

This plant has small leaves and stems. In the fall it turns completely red and can be quite stunning. It grows in a small tree shape and can take on a sort of grove-like appearance. It extends easily and can be left under sunlight all year long.

Sedeveria
(Stonecrops/
Crassulaceae
Family)

Characteristics: A hybrid genus that mixes *Sedum* and *Echeveria*. It combines the cute little leaves of the *Sedum* and the beautiful rosette of the *Echeveria*. Most variants give a very elegant impression.

Cultivation: It really loves sunlight, so place is in a well-lit spot. It's easier to grow outdoors than indoors. It's vital to place it in a well-ventilated spot as well, since it's vulnerable to rotting in summer.

Area of origin: Hybrid Genus

Sedeveria cv. 'Fanfare'

Sedeveria cv. 'Fanfare'

Ventilation ★★★
Light shortage ★★★
Growth rate ★★

The sharp, thin leaves are delicate as well as lovely. The lower leaves wither and grow into new plants, producing a large number of pups that grow in clusters. These normally grow and drop to the ground, forming a dense clump. In the fall, this plant turns pale yellow and becomes thicker.

Graveria
(Stonecrops/
Crassulaceae
Family)

Characteristics: A hybrid genus that mixes *Graptopetalum* and *Echeveria*. It has solid thick, pointy leaves that grow in beautiful rosettes. It's easy to grow and there are many varieties.

Cultivation: It loves sunlight so it's better placed outdoors. Being strong to both cold and hot weather, it's very easy to grow and propagate. Check for insects and remove them immediately when found.

Area of origin: Hybrid Genus

Graveria 'Debbie'

Graveria 'Debbie'

Ventilation ★★
Light shortage ★★★
Growth rate ★★

This variant keeps its pink color all year long, transitioning to only a slightly darker pink during the fall. It's gorgeous when planted in groupings. It's also easy to propagate. The lower leaves wither and grow into new plants. Inadequate sunlight and/or too-frequent watering will cause the pink color to fade.

<table>
<tr><td>

Agave
(Agavaceae
Family)

</td><td>

Characteristics: The leaves are fleshy and have prickly spines along the sides as well as pointy tips. The leaves are also hard and the center leaves close in tightly, giving them a bud-like appearance. It spreads in a beautiful rosette shape. There are many color and shape variations.

Cultivation: Generally, it's very easy to take care of. Be generous when watering. Let it have plenty of sunlight and it will reward you with a beautiful flower.

Area of origin: US, Mexico

</td></tr>
</table>

Agave titanota sp. No.1

A cool-looking species with rusted-iron-like rims that give the plant a very distinctive look. The large, overlapping leaves lend it a commanding presence.

Ventilation ★
Light shortage ★★
Growth rate ★

Agave parryi var. huachucensis

The bluish green skin and brown spines combine for a beautiful look. This plant's main feature is the jagged edge of its leaf. The large leaves contribute to create a powerful-looking rosette.

Agave stricta

Ventilation ★
Light shortage ★★
Growth rate ★

Its leaves are thin and hard. During the growth period the leaves grow longer, into large rosettes. The tips of the leaves are hard, sharp and painful to the touch. Its pale green color gives a bright presence, and the plant has a very strong nature. The *Agave* family works very well as a companion to cacti. But be sure to give it enough space because it grows and spreads widely.

Agave filifera ssp. Schidigera

This unusual species has curly white spines growing on the edge of its leaves. It almost looks as if the leaves were cut by hand around the rim. Since the leaves will spread, it requires some space if planted in a group.

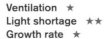

Ventilation ★
Light shortage ★★
Growth rate ★

These plants overlap their leaves in a cross and the leaves themselves come in many shapes. Collecting these plants never gets tiring.

Crassula
(Stonecrops/
Crassulaceae
Family)

Characteristics: These come in many different types, with their main characteristic being the way the leaves overlap in a cross shape if seen from above. The flowers are small but pretty and some of them also have a degree of scent.

Cultivation: They divide in two types: winter type and summer type. The winter type grows in winter and rests in summer and conversely, the summer type grows in summer and rests in winter. Summer types require care to avoid rot, so keep them in a well-ventilated spot.

Area of origin: South and East Africa

Ventilation ★★
Light shortage ★★★
Growth rate ★

Crassula perfoliata var. falcata

The *falcata* was a sword used on the Iberian Peninsula in pre-Roman times, and this plant takes its name from the leaves' resemblance to this ancient blade. Growth is slow but it has a strong nature. Strong sunlight can burn the leaves, so grow in partial/filtered light. It's a summer type of *Crassula*, so avoid planting it along with winter types. Bright, red-orange flowers smelling a bit like cinnamon bloom in the summer.

Crassula 'Ivory Pagoda'

Crassula 'Ivory Pagoda'

This plant has a velvety texture due to the white hair growing on its surface. It's a small variety that grows slowly and produces pup plants in clusters. During warm seasons, if ventilation is lacking, some spots will appear on the surface. It is a winter type.

Ventilation ★★★
Light shortage ★★
Growth rate ★

Crassula cv. 'Kimnachii'

Ventilation ★★★
Light shortage ★★
Growth rate ★

Crassula cv. 'Kimnachii'

Its leaves overlap in a tower shape that gives the plant a wonderfully unique form. The surface is deep green color and covered in hair. It's weak in summer so keep it well-ventilated. It is a winter type.

Crassula remota

Ventilation ★★
Light shortage ★★
Growth rate ★★

Crassula remota

It grows similarly to a vine, and prettily-shaped flowers bloom on its tip. In the fall, the body of the plant turns purple; in the warm seasons it turns silver-colored. During its growth period it grows many pup plants as well. It is a summer type.

Crassula pubescens

Ventilation ★★★
Light shortage ★★★
Growth rate ★★

It is a summer type. In winter it turns a nice red bean color. During warm seasons it changes to a grass-like green instead. The leaves can be removed easily, which makes the cutting process easy as well. Inadequate sunlight can easily cause growth to halt.

Crassula pubescens

Crassula 'Morgan's Beauty'

Crassula 'Morgan's Beauty'

It has thick silver leaves and blooms red flowers during early spring. It's a small plant that spreads its leaves evenly in all four directions. Despite not growing much, it has a strong nature. It is a winter type.

Ventilation ★★★
Light shortage ★★
Growth rate ★

Crassula mesembryanthemoides

Crassula cv. 'Momiji Matsuri'

Crassula cv. 'Momiji Matsuri'

It grows thick, lustrous leaves. Usually green, it becomes a striking red color around the end of fall. It is very strong if exposed to enough sunlight. It also breeds readily during its growth period. It is a summer type.

Ventilation ★
Light shortage ★★★
Growth rate ★★

Crassula mesembryanthemoides

Ventilation ★★★
Light shortage ★★
Growth rate ★★

It has hairy leaves and grows similarly to a tree. The larger it becomes, the more similar it is to a tree. In summer it's silver, with the leaves becoming purple in the fall. It is a summer type.

Crassula hirta

Crassula hirta

Ventilation ★★
Light shortage ★★
Growth rate ★

It grows rosettes with firm, deep green leaves. It is a summer type. The surface of the leaves is rough, and it easily breeds through cutting. It is vulnerable to rotting during summer so be careful. In the picture you can see the flower stem at around 8 inches (20 cm) in length.

Crassula sarmentosa f. variegata

It has a gorgeous red stem with yellow leaves. During the warm seasons, the red color disappears and the plant grows. If not pruned however, it will become messy. Pruned parts can be replanted. It is a summer type.

Ventilation ★★
Light shortage ★★
Growth rate ★★★

Crassula sarmentosa f. variegata

Crassula perforata var. variegata

Crassula perforata var. variegata

Ventilation ★★
Light shortage ★★
Growth rate ★★★

The leaves are thin and medium-sized, and only their edges turn red during the fall. It grows upwards. As it grows the lower part of the stem becomes woody. If you prefer to avoid this, the upper part can be cut to grow a new clean stock. It is a summer type.

Crassula portulacea cv. 'Golum'

Crassula portulacea cv. 'Golum'

Ventilation ★
Light shortage ★★
Growth rate ★★

Has an unusual form, with trumpet-shaped round leaves. This is a hybrid species originally bred from the jade plant (*Crassula Ovata*). The stems grow firmly and the plant becomes full and splendid after three years. It is a summer type.

Crassula mernieriana cv.

Crassula mernieriana cv.

Ventilation ★★★
Light shortage ★★★
Growth rate ★★

The squared leaves seem to be strung along the stem, giving the plant a fun, quirky appearance. It is a summer type. During the fall, only the edges turn red. If it doesn't receive enough sunlight, the distance between the leaves increases and the stems will spread. In group plantings it contributes a sense of movement.

The species covered in hair and sporting bright red patterns are all grouped under the Kalanchoe genus, which is rich in variations and personality.

Kalanchoe
(Stonecrops/
Crassulaceae
Family)

Characteristics: Originally from Madagascar, this genus has many unusual members. Varieties range from small to large, and their leaves can have a pattern, be covered in hair or have a velvety texture. They vary widely in shape as well.

Cultivation: They are very vulnerable to cold in winter. In winter give warm water. If your plant receives enough sunlight, the leaves will grow in a beautiful shape. The variations that have hairy leaves are weak to summer heat and rotting, so keep them well-ventilated.

Area of origin: Madagascar, South Africa

Kalanchoe arborescens

Its leaves are shaped kind of like frogs' feet. It stands erect, and after growing, this plant retains only the leaves on the top of the stem. If given enough time it will grow a tuberous root underground. *Kalanchoe* are vulnerable to cold and must be kept indoors during winter, so it's not recommended to plant them with species that are more dependent on sunlight, such as *sedum*.

Cold weather ★★★
Light shortage ★★★
Growth rate ★★

Kalanchoe hildebrandtii

Kalanchoe hildebrandtii

Ventilation ★★★
Cold weather ★★★
Growth rate ★★

The leaves are smaller than *Kalanchoe bracteate*. Be careful when handling, as the leaves can break off very easily, which also makes cutting for propagating very easy. The surface of the leaves is covered in soft hair. Because of the similarity in their shapes and leaves, *Kalanchoe hildebrandtii* and *Kalanchoe bracteata* are sometimes mistaken for each other.

Kalanchoe bracteata

Kalanchoe orgyalis

Kalanchoe bracteata

Cold weather ★★★
Light shortage ★★★
Growth rate ★★

This plant has spoon-shaped leaves. The whole body is silver, the only exception being the brown edges of the leaves. Because of its shape it's also called "Silver teaspoons." Since the leaves are easy to remove, it's also easy to perform cutting. It also naturally grows many pup plants.

Kalanchoe orgyalis

Cold weather ★★★
Light shortage ★★★
Growth rate ★★

This beautiful plant has chic brown leaves. The lower leaves wither and grow into new plants. When it grows, the leaves become larger and the stems thicker. Due to its dry look, it looks very stylish when planted along with cacti.

Kalanchoe tomentosa

Kalanchoe tomentosa

Ventilation ★★
Cold weather ★★
Growth rate ★★

Also called "Rabbit ears" due to its shape and texture. The brown spots on the edges are called "stars." And leaves with black edges are commonly nicknamed "black rabbit ears."

Kalanchoe tomentosa 'Golden Rabbit'

Kalanchoe beharensis 'Fang'

Kalanchoe tomentosa 'Golden Rabbit'

Ventilation ★★
Cold weather ★★
Growth rate ★★

A variation of *Kalanchoe tomentosa* with yellow leaves. Also called "Golden rabbit." There are other "rabbit" types as well, such as "Black rabbit" or "Wild rabbit." This plant can be easily bred through cutting.

Kalanchoe beharensis 'Fang'

Ventilation ★★★
Cold weather ★★★
Growth rate ★★

The fanglike knobs on the leaves' underside give this plant its nickname. The entire plant, including the stem, is covered in hair. As the plant grows, the leaves also grow in size. It's vulnerable to winter cold, so keep it indoors near sunlight.

Kalanchoe thyrsiflora

Kalanchoe thyrsiflora

This plant has been nicknamed "Flapjacks" because of its charming fan or paddle-shaped leaves. The leaves are covered in white powder and turn completely red during the fall, though occasionally, instead of red, the leaves turn a pure white that is truly beautiful. Inadequate sunlight will halt its growth.

Cold weather ★★★
Light shortage ★★★
Growth rate ★★

Kalanchoe humilis

Kalanchoe humilis

Cold weather ★★
Light shortage ★★
Growth rate ★★

Despite looking a little ferocious, this is a beautiful variety whose color combination and unique leaf pattern make it stand out. It works well as an accent to other plants. It grows a tall flower stalk that looks almost weedy. The plant itself is low-growing.

Aeonium (Stonecrops/ Crassulaceae Family)	**Characteristics**: This genus is very popular for its shape, its wooden stems and the leaves that attach only to the upper part of the stem. Leaf color is usually black or pink, with some yellow variations. Varieties also come in both small and large sizes.

Cultivation: The lower leaves wither and the plant grows upwards. The withering is a normal part of the growth cycle. This genus really likes sunlight, so keep your plants in a well-lit spot.

Area of origin: North Africa, Canary Islands.

Aeonium urbicum cv. 'Sunburst'

Aeonium urbicum cv. 'Sunburst'

Light shortage ★★★
Light intensity ★★
Growth rate ★★

Its leaves grow and spread in beautiful pink, yellow and green colors. The lower leaves wither and the plant grows upwards, retaining only the upper cluster/rosette. The upper part produces seeds to breed the next generation. The plant can also be bred by cutting.

Aeonium urbicum cv. 'Sunburst' cristata

Aeonium urbicum cv. 'Sunburst' cristata

Light intensity ★★★
Light shortage ★★
Growth rate ★★

A type of petrified sunburst that branches into a dense grove. During the growth period, it takes on a beautiful form with pink colored leaves. The withered lower leaves must be removed. If grown along with other plants, it's possible to create a miniature world around it, thanks to its lush, bulky form.

Aeonium spathulatum

Light shortage ★★★
Growth rate ★

This is a small species. The leaves are lovely and include brown-pink shades along with green. Its growth is slow, but when fully grown it becomes a small tree. The leaves are slightly sticky.

Aeonium spathulatum

Aeonium cv. 'Violet Queen'

Aeonium cv. 'Violet Queen'

Ventilation ★★
Light shortage ★★★
Growth rate ★★

A rich, reddish-brown plant with a green center. The fuzz on the surface of the leaves gives a matte impression. It's vulnerable in summer, so keep it in a well-ventilated spot and do not water it.

Aeonium decorum f. variegata

Aeonium decorum f. variegata

Light shortage ★★
Growth rate ★★

The contrast of the yellow, pink and green colors is truly a charming sight. This plant changes color according to the season, with some "plain" periods when it is entirely green. It grows into a lovely tree-like form.

Aeonium arboreum var. atropurpureum

Aeonium arboreum var. atropurpureum

Light shortage ★★
Growth rate ★★

The leaves are black and confined to the top of the stem. When the plant doesn't receive enough light, the leaves green instead, so keep it in a well-lit space. It sheds its leaves in mid-summer and mid-winter and rests for a short period. It adds a chic accent to group plantings.

Bowiea (Lilies/Liliaceae Family)

Characteristics: This is a bulbous genus. Half of the bulb grows underground while its "face" remains above. The sprout grows out of the center of the exposed portion. The bulb sits tight year-round, but the sprout can either wither and grow again with the cycle of seasons, or continue to grow throughout the year, along with the bulb, depending on the variant. During the resting period the plant dies back and goes dormant.

Cultivation: It's strong in nature and easy to grow. There are both summer growth and winter growth types. Continue to water during their resting period. The best growth is achieved by watering regularly during the growth period and keeping and the surrounding area neat and tidy. Given sufficient sunlight, they will produce flowers. You can also harvest seeds from them, from which to grow new plants.

Area of origin: South Africa

Bowiea volubilis

Light shortage ★★
Growth rate ★★

Also called "Climbing onion," its stems and leaves are similar to seaweed and gradually grow during the growing season. The larger the bulb, the faster the stem will grow.

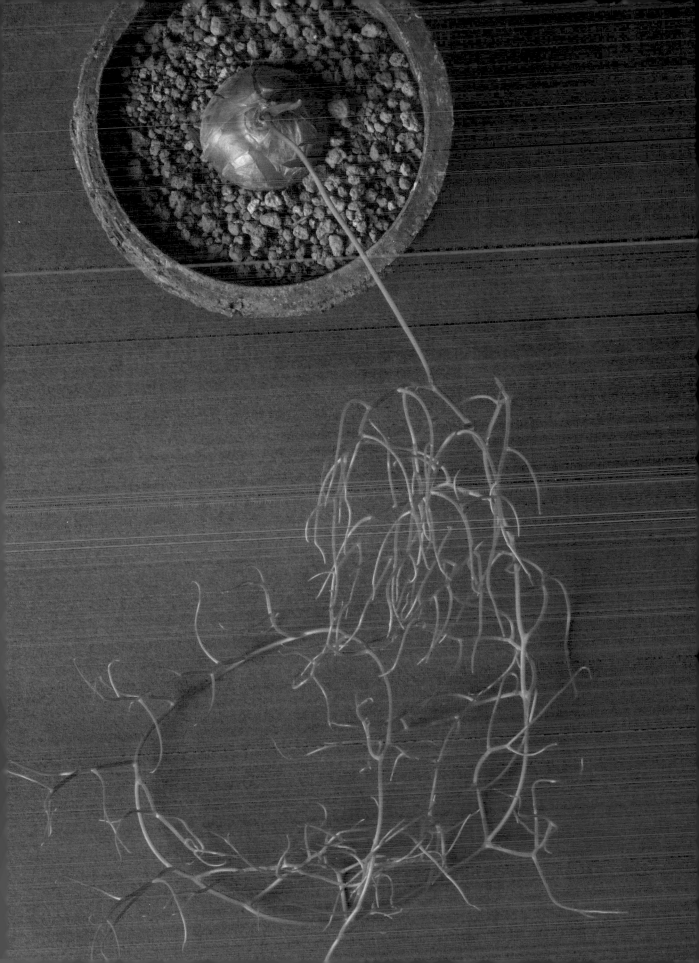

Portulacaria (Purslanes/ Portulacenae Family)	**Characteristics**: These plants have thick stems somewhat similar to tree trunks, so they don't really look like succulents. However, in Africa they grow naturally, accumulating water on their stems and leaves. In nature, this genus looks rather like a bush and is often eaten by elephants.

Cultivation: It is extremely vulnerable to cold weather. In winter it must be grown indoors. It likes sun.

Area of origin: South Africa

Portulacaria afra var. variegata

Cold weather ★★★
Strong of sunlight ★★★
Growth rate ★★

This plant is often called "Rainbow bush" or "Elephant bush." Its leaves form a lovely pattern. The stems extend in all four directions. Given adequate sunlight, the rim of each leaf turns a beautiful pink. When fully grown the stems are very thick. The plant can be tended by pruning and so on in a fashion similar to bonsai.

Portulacaria afra var. variegata

Portulacaria molokiniensis

Portulacaria molokiniensis

Cold weather ★★★
Strong of sunlight ★★★
Growth rate ★

Its growth is very slow, and leaves grow only on the upper part of the stem. Since it's vulnerable to cold temperatures, absolutely keep indoors during winter. The thicker the stem gets, the larger the leaves become.

Adenia
(Passion flowers/
Passifloraceae
Family)

Characteristics: This is a tuber genus. Their stem has the shape of a *sake* bottle and it stores water. The branches shoot from the stem, growing during warmer seasons and resturing during the cold seasons. In the cold periods, the branches withre and fall, leaving only the tuberous stem. In spring the sprouts shoot up and grow again, a sure sign that a new season has begun. Unless grown from seeds, the stems do not grow into their charcteristic *sake* bottle shape.

Cultivation: Avoid watering during the resting season in winter and keep it in a warm place. If properly left without water, it will easily survive the winter. During growth season, water regularly and let it grow naturally.

Area of origin: Asia, Africa

Adenia glauca

Cold weather ★★★
Growth rate ★

The shape and drape of its leaves give it a quirky charm. It grows yellow flowers. If the stem grows too long, it might break because of its weight, so a consider placing a supporting pole next to it to help it hold together.

Gasteria
(Lilies/Liliaceae
Family)

Characteristics: They have deep green, fleshy leaves and a rather harsh presence. They are many variants, some with rough textures on the surface of the leaves and some with grotesque patterns. Since the shape of the flower looks somewhat like a stomach, this genus's name derives from the Latin word for stomach—*gaster*.

Cultivation: It's very resistant to both cold and hot weather, making it easy to grow, even in weak sunlight. It's best grown indoors next to windows. Since the roots are thick, leaves can be kept neat and tidy all year long through regular watering.

Area of origin: South Africa

Gasteria armstrongii

Light intensity ★★
Growth rate ★

This plant grows in the shape of a cow's tongue. Since there are many variants, it's very popular among collectors. The deep, dark green color can be maintained by growing the plant in shade. Due to its thick roots, it's vulnerable to drought, so water regularly all year long.

Gasteria glomerate

Light intensity ★★
Growth rate ★

From the slightly silver tint and rough texture of its surface to its plump, misshapen flowers, this plant is full of interesting features. This is a dwarf species that grows in clusters. Its leaves are pretty thick and firm. If exposed too much to sunlight, it'll get sunburned and turn brown. The plant in the picture has a foot-long (30 cm) flower stem.

<table>
<tr><td>

Senecio
(Daisy/
Asteraceae
Family)

</td><td>

Characteristics: Its main characteristic is its "green necklace" look. It comes in a number of colors and shapes, from variants that hang downwards to those that grow vertically. The leaf patterns are also very varied. Its flowers have an unusual smell, similar to that of dandelions.

</td></tr>
</table>

Cultivation: It likes water. It's vulnerable to rotting during summer; however, don't let the roots become completely dry. Water regularly but in moderation. The strong mid-summer sunlight will cause sunburn, but be careful to not place the plants in complete shade as that will halt the plant's growth.

Area of origin: South-west Africa

Senecio haworthii

Senecio haworthii

Light shortage ★★
Light intensity ★★★
Ventilation ★★★

Leaves and stems are covered in white hair. The shape of the leaves has earned it the nickname "Cocoon plant." This plant is very vulnerable to rotting in summer so be sure to provide good ventilation and refrain from watering. Despite becoming thinner during summer, it gradually recovers in the fall after receiving water. It is not suitable for planting alongside other plants.

Senecio crassissimus

Senecio crassissimus

Cold weather ★★★
Light shortage ★★
Growth rate ★★

The leaves of this plant grow vertically, so that their flat surfaces are not exposed to full sun. In the fall it turns a beautiful purple color. It is vulnerable to cold.

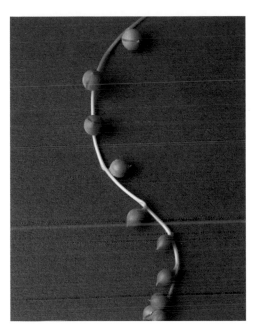

Senecio rowleyanus

Ventilation ★★★
Light intensity ★★★
Growth rate ★★★

Also called "String of pearls," this a species that has been popular since ancient times, with its charming shape consisting of round leaves attached to a long stem. In group plantings it adds a lovely sense of movement. It will wither if not watered often, and thus requires care against rotting all year long. Place it in a well-ventilated spot and water regularly, possibly on chilly evenings for best results.

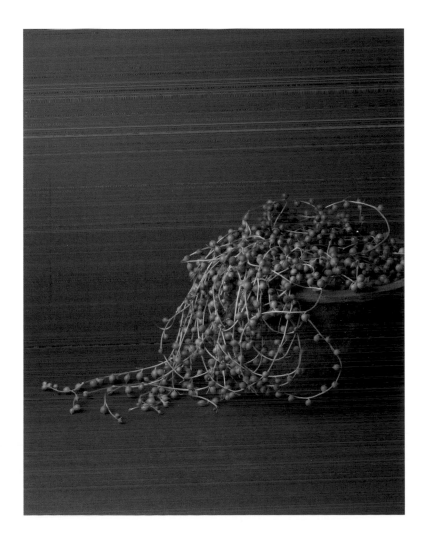

Spines

Succulent plants that have spines but are not cacti. The spines are flowers that have changed over time through evolution, and the epidermis of these plants is deformed because of that.

Euphorbia (Spurges/ Euphorbiaceae Family)

Characteristics: There are many variants under this name. Their common characteristic is their beautiful green body. Despite having spines, they do not have areoles on the surface, which excludes them from the cacti family. Plants in this genus are popular among collectors for their many shapes. When touched they release a glue-like liquid, a defense mechanism to protect them from insects and animals.

Cultivation: If regular watering stops, its growth also comes to a complete halt, and even if watering is resumed afterwards, it takes a long time to start growing again. Therefore, give water all year long. It's vulnerable to cold weather, so in winter months, grow it indoors in a warm environment. Place in a well-ventilated spot during summer to avoid rot.

Area of origin: Africa, Madagascar

Euphorbia horrida

Ventilation ★ ★
Cold weather ★ ★
Growth rate ★ ★

Also called "African milk barrel," this plant has a beautiful silver skin. The lower part is wooden, rather like a tree trunk. It drops seedlings that grow in clusters. The spines are actually the remnants of flower stems, and are quite rigid.

Euphorbia bupleurifolia cv. 'Kaimagyoku'

Ventilation ★★
Cold weather ★★★
Growth rate ★

Euphorbia enopla

Ventilation ★★
Cold weather ★★★
Growth rate ★

Euphorbia bupleurifolia cv. 'Kaimagyoku'

A hybrid species derived from *Euphorbia bupleurifolia* and *Euphorbia gabisan*, it has a lovely pineapple shape. It usually grows leaves only on the top section. Once it becomes relatively large, it starts growing pup plants.

Euphorbia enopla

Red spines make a beautiful contrast to the green body. If it doesn't receive enough water, the spines turn black and stop growing. Watering regularly all year long keeps the spines nice and healthy. It has a strong presence in group plantings, so give it a leading role in your arrangement.

Euphorbia bupleurifolia

Euphorbia bupleurifolia

This plant uses its rock-shaped body as a water tank. The leaves grow only on top of the tank, similarly to the pineapple it resembles. The leaves are thin and appear only during growth, and fall during winter.

Ventilation ★★★
Cold weather ★★★
Growth rate ★

Euphorbia trigona

Euphorbia trigona

Leafy as well as thorny, this plant is also called "African milk tree." It's popular as an indoor plant, but be sure to give adequate sunlight; insufficient exposure will cause it to grow thin and slowly.

Ventilation ★★
Cold weather ★★
Growth rate ★★

Euphorbia mammillaris cv. 'Variegata'

An unusual species that is kind of reptilian in appearance. During the growing season it sports pink leaves. If watered too often, it will not grow properly, so water moderately during the growing season. Once grown, it will start growing en masse from the upper part.

Euphorbia mammillaris cv. 'Variegata'

Euphorbia ferox

Euphorbia ferox

Ventilation ★★
Cold weather ★★
Growth rate ★★

This small species has beautiful purple spines. Despite its small size, it breeds and grows pup plants all around itself. The lower part will easily turn woody. If it's planted alongside similar plants (such as any *Euphorbia* or *Haorsia*), the color of the spines adds a very nice accent.

Euphorbia echinus

Euphorbia echinus

Ventilation ★★
Cold weather ★★
Growth rate ★

This is a rough dwarf species with several ridges. It extends vertically like a pillar cactus. The lower part of the stem will easily turn woody; this is a natural part of its growth.

Euphorbia enopla ver.

Euphorbia enopla ver.

Ventilation ★★
Cold weather ★★
Growth rate ★

This is one of the spiniest species, earning it the nickname "Pincushion *Euphorbia*." Some of its spines are red/orange—these grow thicker than others on the plant. It's vulnerable to cold weather, so keep it indoors during winter.

Pachypodium (Dogbanes/ Apocynaceae Family)	**Characteristics**: Its thick silver stems are full of water. Only the stem remains during the winter, but in spring it grows flowers and thick leaves.

Cultivation: Weak to cold, they shed their leaves in winter. During this time, let them rest in a warm place and do not water. Once the weather gets warmer, they will start growing new leaves. Start watering only after the leaves appear.

Area of origin: Africa, Madagascar

Pachypodium rosulatum

Cold weather ★★★
Light shortage ★
Growth rate ★★

Also called "Elephant's foot," this plant has pale green elliptical leaves that appear in the growing season and drop during the colder months. It puts out long shoots from which bloom beautiful yellow flowers during spring. It's vulnerable to cold weather, so keep indoors during winter. It grows very slowly, but doesn't attract insects, so it's easy to grow. The picture shows the appearance of new leaves; these grow bigger during summer.

PART 2

Unique Cactus Species

Cacti are also succulent plants. There are many sub families (such as *Astrophytum* or *Mammillaria*) but they generally all belong under the Cactus family. The common characteristic of all plants in the cactus family is the presence of an "areole" at the base of each spine. Most are leafless, storing moisture in their stems, which are protected by a waxy cuticle. In this chapter, I will introduce many unique cacti, for example those with a charming form or with an unusual or rare skin.

This is what they look like when fully grown! Only in a botanical garden or native habitat will you see a plant reach this size.

They also grow in amusing shapes.

Photo: Kawaguchi Green Center, Saitama Prefecture, Kawaguchi City.

Let's observe some large cacti at a botanical garden

Botanical gardens offer a great opportunity to see a wide variety of succulents and cacti. Their greenhouses may contain some wonderful rare plants.

From top to bottom: A bush of *Mammillaria*. They grow in beautiful clusters that give a sense of their original home.

These *Lilacina* are growing beautifully.

These Golden barrels (*Echinocactus grusonii*) are around 20 to 30 years old and have very strong spines.

Some succulents and cacti have interesting nicknames owing to their quirky looks. For example, the genus below is often called "Button cactus" and "Pingpong ball" cactus owing to their shapes. They have other nicknames in other parts of the world as well.

Epithelantha (Cactus/ Cactaceae Family)

Characteristics: Its pudgy little body is completely covered in short white spines that form a tuft at the tip. This is a small species, and generally slow-growing. As it grows, it produces fluffy hair in the middle of the areole, with shiny pink flowers on top. Most of its variants breed by expelling seedlings. The shape they take, with many heads popping out of the ground, is quirky but appealing, giving a sort of spore-like atmosphere.

Cultivation: Growth is very slow, but if care is taken during summer heat, they are generally easy to grow. In summer refrain from watering and place it in a well-ventilated spot. When watering, only water the bottom part and do not pour water on the flowers. By watering correctly, the hair will become healthy and fluffy.

Area of origin: Mexico

Epithelantha bokei

In Japan this is also called "Child's hat." Despite very slow growth and extreme vulnerability to heat, its charm is unrivaled. It doesn't breed on its own. To produce a new generation, cut the trunk and replant the growing points in a small group. This plant is highlighted by the spines that cover its entire surface.

Ventilation ★★★
Light shortage ★★★
Growth rate ★

Epithelantha micromeris

Ventilation ★★★
Light shortage ★★★
Growth rate ★

This species is also called "Moon world" in Japan. It grows a large number of pups, which help give it its characteristic shape, consisting of multiple stems growing together. It takes time to grow the whole cluster. Keep it in a well-lit spot during growth. Its flowers are followed by a tuft of little red fruits. It looks great if planted alongside other cacti.

Lophophora (Cactus/ Cactaceae Family)

Characteristics: They have a cute shape, rather like that of a steamed bun. Instead of spines, they grow plenty of delightful hair. The hair in the center is the flower's seat. The hair divides and blooms into small flowers. The matte texture of their skin is reminiscent of the dry weather of their native Mexico.

Cultivation: This variety grows so slowly that you may sometimes wonder if your plant is still alive. Despite being easy to grow, growing it in a nice neat shape is fairly challenging. To keep its plump and round form, water very slightly in summer. Keep it in a well-ventilated place, as it will otherwise rot. To keep the hair fluffy, absolutely avoid getting water on it.

Area of origin: Mexico

Lophophora diffusa

Ventilation ★★★
Light shortage ★★
Growth rate ★

It expands in a plump shape. Its skin is a nice, pale green shade similar to jade. It has a lot of hair in the middle and if the hair is fluffy enough it will bloom flowers. Give good ventilation to prevent rot.

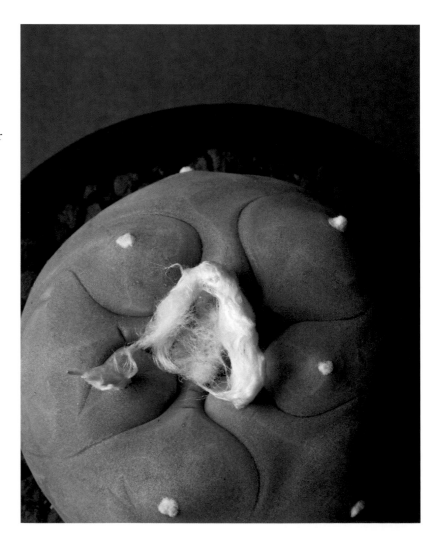

Lophophora diffusa

Lophophora diffusa

Ventilation ★★★
Light shortage ★★
Growth rate ★

This species has a lot of variations, and this particular plant shows a larger body, stronger green color and more hair. As with all plants in this genus, the hair will be nicer if water is kept away from it.

Lophophora williamsii
(Peyote)

Ventilation ★★★
Light shortage ★
Growth rate ★

The celadon colored skin is covered in white powder, and its flowers are pink. It is strong but has a very slow growth. When it grows older, it starts to breed for new generations. The type that reproduces asexually is called germinating peyote. Please note that in some parts of the world peyote is illegal or heavily restricted.

Lophophora williamsii

Espostoa (Cactus/Cactaceae Family)	**Characteristics:** These pillar cacti are covered in white hair. The manner of hair growth depends on the variant, but the common point among all variants is the shaggy texture. This genus is originally from the very cold mountains of Peru, and the hairy surface evolved as protection from cold in the winter and from strong sunlight in the warmer months. It's a wonderful example of the plant world's ability to survive and thrive.

Cultivation: They are relatively strong, however they also wither easily if they don't receive enough water. In summer they are vulnerable to rotting so keep them well-ventilated.

Area of origin: Peru

Espostoa melanostele

Ventilation ★ ★ ★
Light shortage ★
Growth rate ★

This plant is nicknamed "Peruvian old lady" because of its stately presence and long white hair. It grows vertically, becoming a pillar cactus. The hair wraps around it to provide protection. Interspersed in the hairs are firm spines. Its form and color make it stand out in group plantings and can both blend and contrast very nicely.

<table>
<tr><td>

Echinofossulocactus
(Cactus/Cactaceae
Family)

</td><td>

Characteristics: Members of this genus go by names like "Wave cactus" and "Brain cactus" and other nicknames. Their folds help increase surface area, making it more optimal for photosynthesis, as well as creating shadows that help regulate body temperature. Most variants are spherical with beautiful spines.

</td></tr>
</table>

Cultivation: They are easy to grow and very strong. If placed in a well-lit spot and watered regularly all year long, they will grow in a nice form and have beautiful spines. They also easily get sunburned, so during summer when light is strong, water slightly more often and regularly.

Area of origin: Mexico

Echinofossulocactus multicostatus

Echinofossulocactus multicostatus
(also known as *Stenocactus multicostatus*)

Ventilation ★
Light intensity ★
Growth rate ★

This species blooms purple striped flowers during spring. When the plants are young and small, the flower can grow large enough to upstage the plant's charming green body. The body grows large and has large waves. The surface is smooth, flat and hard. It combines well with other cacti in group plantings.

Echinofossulocactus multicostatus f. elegans

Echinofossulocactus multicostatus f. elegans

Ventilation ★
Light intensity ★
Growth rate ★

Deep wrinkles, bright green body and yellow spines give this plant plenty of eye appeal. Do plant with other green cacti, but avoid combining with other cacti that have white spines.

These cacti are wonderful not only for their colors and shapes, but also for the unusual textures of their skins. Some have a texture similar to the skin of reptiles, while others have spotted patterns.

Astrophytum
(Cactus/
Cactaceae
Family)

Characteristics: The name of this genus means "star plant" in Greek—an apt designation, as the patterns on the plants' skins often suggest a starry sky, and their shape is often similar to a star. They have no spines. They bloom with a large yellow flower in the center. The flowers leave behind them a pattern that creates an attractive design.

Cultivation: While their growth is quite slow, they are easy to grow and strong in nature. In summer avoid direct strong sunlight; rather, place it in partial shade and in a well-ventilated spot to prevent rotting.

Area of origin: Mexico

Astrophytum myriostigma var. quadricostatum

This specific variant spreads in four conical shapes. There is a variant that spreads in three shapes called *tricostatum*. The original plant usually spreads in five conical shapes. While still a somewhat rare plant, they are easier to obtain than they once were. Being a very unique species, these plants really should be appreciated on their own rather than in groups.

Ventilation ★★★
Light intensity ★★★
Growth rate ★

Astrophytum myriostigma

Ventilation ★★★
Light shortage ★★★
Growth rate ★

The pattern on the skin is filled with "stars" —so many of them that the plant most looks solid white in color. This plant grows in a vertical column shape. Its miter-like form has earned it the nickname "Bishop's cap." A large yellow flower blooms in the center of the cactus in early summer.

 →

Characteristics: They bloom beautiful large yellow flowers, but the bulging flower buds are what's truly attractive in the plants of this family. Although there's a lot of variation in the color of spines, the main characteristic of this species is the round shape of the cactus.

Cultivation: It's easy to grow and very strong. As long as the plant receives enough sunlight, the flowers will almost certainly bloom each year. The beauty of the flowers will increase year by year, especially if the plant is fertilized after the flowering season is over.

Area of origin: Brazil

Notocactus mammulosus var.
(*Parodia mammulosa* variant)

Ventilation ★
Light shortage ★★
Growth rate ★

The center is a bit hollow, with an interesting flat shape that acts as a container for the plant's flowers. The maculated body becomes pretty large and assumes a leading role when planted in a group. This has a strong nature and personality and grows well alongside other plants.

Notocactus mammulosus var.

Notocactus scopa

Notocactus scopa
(also called *Parodia scopa*)

Ventilation ★
Light shortage ★★
Growth rate ★

It has a beautiful round shape covered in fluffy white hair. The spines can be red, as pictured here, but there are also variants with white spines. There's even a variant with spiral-shaped pines. After growing in a large spherical shape, it starts becoming vertical/cylindrical. Its growth is slightly faster than other *Notocactus* and it grows without releasing seedlings.

<table>
<tr><td>

Thelocactus
(Cactus/
Cactaceae
Family)

</td><td>

Characteristics: This genus has very strong spines and large flowers. There are many variants with different colored or shaped spines. Instead of releasing seeds, their maculated bodies grow vertically into pillars.

Cultivation: The spines are strong and their color is healthy if the plant receives strong sunlight. When the plant is too dry, the spine color fades, so water regularly. These plants are also very vulnerable to rot in summer, so keep them in a well-ventilated spot.

Area of origin: Mexico, U.S.

</td></tr>
</table>

Thelocactus macdowellii

Thelocactus macdowellii

Ventilation ★
Light shortage ★★
Growth rate ★

Its long, white spines and pink flowers that are very beautiful. The most striking characteristic is arrangement of the longer needle-like spines and shorter spines, creating a pleasing overall shape. In the case of small seedlings, only the shorter spines appear. This plant can self-pollinate.

Thelocactus heterochromus

Ventilation ★
Light shortage ★★
Growth rate ★

The spines have a gradient color that goes from white to red. The flower can grow very large, to the point that it completely obscures the body of the plant itself. The flower blooms only for two or three days, which is a pity.

Thelocactus heterochromus

59

Gymnocalycium (Cactus/Cactaceae Family)

Characteristics: Most of the species in this genus are rough, but there are also some with round details and thin shapes. The skin looks similar to reptile skin and feels very fresh. Their main attraction is their big, beautiful multilayered flower. The flower's color can vary from white to dark pink.

Cultivation: They are easy to grow, and can grow in relatively low light. Keep watering and place in a well-ventilated spot all year long, so that the skin will stay fresh and clean. If your plant stops growing and the skin loses its gloss, give it plenty of water until it recovers.

Area of origin: South Africa, South America

Gymnocalycium mihanovichii var. friedrichii cv. 'Hibotan Nishiki'

Ventilation ★
Light shortage ★★
Growth rate ★★

This is a variant of *Gymnocalycium mihanovichii var. friedrichii*, with spots. The red color indicates the loss of the original pigment due to mutation. This species has many fans, due to its large variety of colors. When watered regularly, its fresh skin resembles that of a reptile. It also produces wonderful flowers.

Gymnocalycium baldianum

Ventilation ★
Light shortage ★★
Growth rate ★★

Also called "Chin cactus," it has a lovely deep green skin and beautifully-spaced starburst spines. It blooms magnificent flowers that range from white to pale pink, vivid pink, scarlet or purple. If it doesn't receive enough water, the skin loses its firmness and becomes squishy, so water regularly all year long. Its nature is very strong and it's easy to grow.

Gymnocalycium baldianum

Gymnocalycium baldianum f. monst

Gymnocalycium baldianum f. monst

Ventilation ★
Light shortage ★★
Growth rate ★★

A crested variant of *Gymnocalycium baldianum*. It's very expensive due to its rarity. It easily grows lots of flowers of varying bright colors. It should not be watered from the top but directly at the base, so that water doesn't accumulate in the hollow part of the center.

Chamaecereus
(Cactus/
Cactaceae
Family)

Characteristics: There is only one species in this family: *Chamaecereus silvestrii*. This species is mostly popular for breeding with other cacti. It blooms multiple deep orange flowers.

Cultivation: It's resistant to both cold and hot weather, and can therefore be grown outdoors all year long. It loves sunlight. If kept cool during winter, it can receive little to no water during those months, depending on the level of cold. And if allowed to rest in this way, the following flowering period will be all the more glorious.

Area of origin: Argentina

Chamaecereus silvestrii

Chamaecereus silvestrii

Ventilation ★★★
Light shortage ★★
Growth rate ★★

This plant has a short, slender, wriggling form. The stem is only about ¼–½ inch (1 cm) thick and produces plenty of pup plants. It is stringy, to the point of overflowing and hanging over the edge of the container. It produces many beautiful, deep orange flowers. While this plant is good for breeding, it's not suited to combining with other plants.

Eriocactus
(Cactus/
Cactaceae
Family)

Characteristics: These start out as a sphere; then, when their diameter is large enough, they start growing vertically in a column. Some species start breeding even before becoming vertical. Flowers do not bloom until the plant achieves its cylindrical in shape.

Cultivation: They are strong and slow-growing. If they don't receive enough sunlight, their growth will be even slower. In order to form into a pillar as it grows, the lower part of the plant dies and becomes woody.

Area of origin: Brazil

Eriocactus leninghausii

Eriocactus leninghausii
(**also called** *Parodia leninghausii*)

Ventilation ★
Light shortage ★★
Growth rate ★★

This plant has several nicknames, including "Yellow tower" and "Lemon ball." In addition to its bristly golden spines, which can grow long and graceful, this plant also produces a lovely yellow flower once it reaches its cylindrical shape.

<table>
<tr><td>

Echinocereus
(Cactus/
Cactaceae
Family)

</td><td>

Characteristics: These are very popular, as many species of this genus grow flowers large enough to cover the plant's entire body. When compared to their gorgeous flowers, their bodies tend to look rather plain. There are many varieties and they produce a wonderful variety of flowers.

Cultivation: They are a very strong species. However, their flowers will not bloom unless they are watered regularly and placed in well-lit spots all year long. Especially during winter, make sure the plant gets plenty of sunlight to ensure blooming in the spring.

Area of origin: Mexico

</td></tr>
</table>

Echinocereus pentalophus

Echinocereus pentalophus

Ventilation ★★
Light shortage ★★
Growth rate ★★

Also called "Ladyfinger cactus," this plant produces magenta flowers that grow profusely, even if they bloom for only a couple of weeks. Branches are slender, finger-like and often tightly grouped. They can grow erect or can sprawl. After the flowers bloom, the plant becomes thirstier, so water it more often than previously. It's recommended for beginners, as it is a very easy plant to grow.

Echinocereus rigidissimus

Echinocereus rigidissimus

Ventilation ★★★
Light shortage ★★
Growth rate ★

This is a curly type, with purple spines. It's also nicknamed "Rainbow hedgehog" as, seen from above, it looks like an adorable curled-up creature. Vivid purplish-pink flowers appear in spring and can grow large enough to hide the plant's body. Its growth is very slow and steady.

<table>
<tr><td>

Opuntia
(Cactus/
Cactaceae
Family)

</td><td>

Characteristics: Plants in this genus have nicknames like "Prickly pear" and "Paddle cactus," as their pads are flat and typically rounded. Despite having small spines, they stick immediately to the skin when touched, so be careful when handling them. The flowers do not bloom until the cactus grows considerably.

</td></tr>
</table>

Cultivation: They are very strong in nature and grow well. If they don't receive enough sunlight, they will grow vertically quickly, rather than hold onto their spherical shape for any length of time. If they don't receive enough water, they droop and become shriveled; if this occurs, water regularly and more often. They are resilient to both cold and hot weather. In addition, one of the sections can be cut and used to easily breed new generations.

Area of origin: Mexico

Opuntia rubescens

Ventilation ★
Light shortage ★★★
Growth rate ★★

A beautiful species with a rough green body. Its flat, long and slender shape has grace and charm. During growth it is very thirsty. If kept in a well-lit spot, it grows without any tapering toward the end of the body.

Opuntia rubescens

Opuntia microdasys var. albispina

Opuntia microdasys var. albispina

Ventilation ★★
Light shortage ★★★
Growth rate ★★

This plant has beautiful white and fluffy spines, but despite its cute looks those spines really hurt, so be careful! Common nicknames for this plant are "Angel wings" and "Bunny ears." When planted with other plants, it takes the lead, with its strong presence and charming appearance.

Echinocactus
(Cactus/
Cactaceae
Family)

Characteristics: This genus grows a large spherical body. It is emblematic of Mexico, which is its area of origin. The spines are very sharp and beautiful. These plants don't grow flowers until they reach a very large size, which can take up to 30 years to achieve. After the first bloom however, they grow beautiful yellow flowers every year.

Cultivation: They are very strong and easy to grow. Place them in a well-lit spot. They grow beautiful, firm spines if exposed to sunlight and watered regularly.

Area of origin: Mexico

Echinocactus grusonii

Echinocactus grusonii

Ventilation ★
Light shortage ★★
Growth rate ★

This plant is also called "Golden barrel cactus," as the spines and flowers are both a beautiful yellow. It has a slow growth period during which it cannot be bred. When fully grown it can reach 14–20 inches (35–50 cm) in diameter! The tip has a flower bed in the center, but this plant tends to be grown as foliage, as the flowers are disproportionately small.

Tephrocactus
(Cactus/
Cactaceae
Family)

Characteristics: A genus still apparently in the process of evolution, on the threshold of having a flat, thin body like *Opuntia*. They grow as a series of spherical or egg-shaped bodies. In order to breed more easily, the seedlings grow in a way that is easy for them to hitch a ride on passing animals and be deposited elsewhere. Their growth is extremely slow and steady.

Cultivation: They are very strong and easy to grow. Their growth is so slow they might seem dead, but don't worry; they don't actually wither. When they receive insufficient water they become wrinkly. If this occurs, water them regularly until they recover.

Area of origin: Argentina

Tephrocactus articulatus

Tephrocactus articulatus

Ventilation ★
Light shortage ★★
Growth rate ★

The stem nodes grow in a spherical shape and grow a new sphere each year. Each spherical node is easily removed, so be careful— if the plant grows to a very large size, these nodes can fall off with the slightest touch. The plant grows white, semi-transparent flat spines. The skin is silver in color.

Flowers These species grow incredibly beautiful flowers despite their form. When these flowers open, it's like receiving a gift from these wonderful plants.

Brasilicactus
(Cactus/
Cactaceae
Family)

Characteristics: This genus has only two varieties that differ in flower color. The flowers are either bright orange or green. The flowers are large, and one of them will tend to survive for much longer than the others, prolonging the pleasure in looking at them. It's delightful to see the many flowers growing at once.

Cultivation: They are a relatively strong variety, but are very vulnerable to rot in summer. During summer, keep them in a well-ventilated area and water regularly. They also really like sunlight; if kept indoors, they stop growing and the flowers will be of poor quality. To prevent this, keep your plants in a well-lit spot all year long. This genus attracts aphids so check your plants often.

Area of origin: Brazil

Brasilicactus haselbergii

Ventilation ★★★
Light shortage ★★
Growth rate ★★

Round and fat like a ball, this cactus is covered in soft white spines. It grows multiple beautiful, bright orange flowers that look magnificent when planted alongside other cacti. It grows in a nice, even shape. It does not grow in clusters. Place in a well-lit spot.

<table>
<tr><td>

Sulcorebutia
(Cactus/
Cactaceae
Family)

</td><td>

Characteristics: The charm of this genus comes from large flowers that bloom in generous numbers and vary in color, ranging from red to yellow. Most of the species under this genus are small in size but grow in clusters and spread widely.

Cultivation: During their growth they need plenty of water. Water often and place them in a well-lit spot to help them grow nice and firm.

Area of origin: South America

</td></tr>
</table>

Ventilation ★★
Light shortage ★★
Growth rate ★★

Sulcorebutia candiae

Long silver spines densely cover the body of this species. It grows multiple beautiful orange flowers. Once it grows to a certain point, it starts spreading a new generation around itself, growing offspring in clusters. Bear these clusters in mind when planting this cactus in a group, and be sure to allow them adequate growing space.

 Areole The part from which spines grow on cacti is called the areole. These species are covered in areole with spines that look like fluffy, piled-up snow.

> *Mammillaria*
> (Cactus/
> Cactaceae
> Family)

Characteristics: This genus includes many species, from smaller-sized varieties to very large ones. Since the areole tend to look like warts, plants in this genus are also nicknamed "Wart cactus." They grow many small crown-shaped flowers every year. The smaller-sized species are extremely popular, as they grow lovely flowers despite their small size.

Cultivation: They grow fast compared to most other cacti. In order to keep them round, they must be placed in well-lit spots, especially during their growth periods. If the plants receive plenty of sunlight throughout the year, the quality and shape of the flowers will improve massively. They are also very vulnerable to rot in summer, so be sure their space is also well-ventilated. They are relatively resilient to cold in winter.

Area of origin: Mexico

Mammillaria elongata var. albispina

Ventilation ★ ★ ★
Light shortage ★★★
Growth rate ★★

It grows in groups of cylindrical thumb-sized sections. Its lovely golden spines appear on most variations of *mammillaria*. The small pale yellow flowers bloom only on the upper side of the cactus. It's very easy to grow, and it looks striking when planted with similar species that have different spine colors.

Mammillaria martinezii

Mammillaria martinezii

This plant is small and round and covered completely in short white spines. In winter it blooms a crown of dark pink flowers. These are small but grow well and are hardy. The plant rises in a cylindrical shape.

Ventilation ★★★
Light shortage ★★★
Growth rate ★★

Mammillaria brauneana

Mammillaria glassii var. ascensionis

Ventilation ★★★
Light shortage ★★★
Growth rate ★

Mammillaria brauneana

It grows round and squat in shape, and produces a large flower with a pink striped pattern. Although its growth is very slow, it's easy to manage and grows strong.

Ventilation ★★★
Light shortage ★★★
Growth rate ★★

Mammillaria glassii var. ascensionis

This beautiful species grows in clusters. The plants have fluffy white radial spines and brilliant pale flowers that bloom in winter. Its central spines can be straight or curved.

Mammillaria herrerae

Mammillaria herrerae

Ventilation ★★★
Light shortage ★★★
Growth rate ★

This plant has uniformly curved spines. Its dark pink flower is large and shoots out from between the spines. It's very vulnerable to summer rot, so keep well-ventilated.

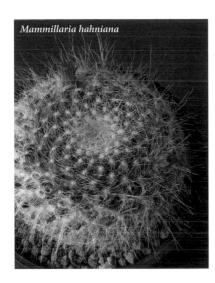
Mammillaria hahniana

Mammillaria hahniana

It has fluffy long hair with short spines. Its flowers bloom in the shape of a crown. As it grows larger, it also grows longer hair that ultimately covers its entire body. Be careful when watering and make sure the spines don't get wet.

Ventilation ★ ★ ★
Light shortage ★ ★ ★
Growth rate ★ ★

Mammillaria spinosissima cv. 'Un Pico'

Ventilation ★ ★ ★
Light shortage ★ ★ ★
Growth rate ★ ★

Mammillaria spinosissima cv. 'Un Pico'

The long, straight white spines of this plant look rather like quills. It is a hybrid species, so it has a resilient nature and is also easy to grow. Rather than expelling seedlings, it simply grows in a large spherical shape.

Mammillaria zeilmanniana

Ventilation ★ ★ ★
Light shortage ★ ★ ★
Growth rate ★ ★

Mammillaria zeilmanniana

This plant flowers very easily. It starts producing lush flowers even when it'ssmall. Be careful of the hook-shaped spines. Since it grows fast, remember to leave some space around it when planting it near other plants.

Mammillaria bocasana roseiflora

Ventilation ★ ★ ★
Light shortage ★ ★ ★
Growth rate ★ ★

Flowers range from a soft pink to a glossy pink-beige, and the shaggy look of the spines matches the flowers beautifully. After it grows past a certain point, this cactus starts growing the next generation around itself in a cluster. Keep it in a well-ventilated spot during summer, as it's quite vulnerable to rotting.

Mammillaria bocasana roseiflora

Ventilation ★★★
Light shortage ★★★
Growth rate ★

Mammillaria humboldtii var. caespitosa

Its growth is very slow. A solitary sphere can seem a bit too minimal; once it grows into a large colony, it's truly a splendid sight. Despite their small bodies, these spheres produce plenty of large, dark pink flowers. Its white spines are little and delicate.

Mammillaria marksiana

Unlike most species of *Mammillaria*, instead of pink flowers on top of white spines, *Mammillaria marksiana* grows golden flowers on top of yellow spines, and grows white hair in-between its warts.

Ventilation ★★★
Light shortage ★★★
Growth rate ★★

Mammillaria elongata f. monst

Ventilation ★★★
Light shortage ★★★
Growth rate ★★

A crested variant of *Mammillaria elongate*. It appears to be growing in all directions, giving the impression of tentacle movement. It tends to sprawl and spread.

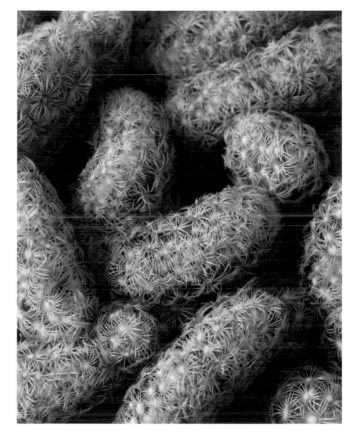

Mammillaria candida var. rosea

This plant usually grows to a very large size in a single spherical shape, without producing seedlings or growing new generations. However, in rare cases, it does grow pups. It blooms with beautiful pink-striped white flowers. Its spines can be tinged with pink as well.

Mammillaria elongata f. monst

Mammillaria candida var. rosea

Ventilation ★★★
Light shortage ★★★
Growth rate ★

These cacti originate from rainforests and have a form that attaches itself to trees and hangs down. In order to attach themselves anywhere, they have small roots growing all over the stem.

Rhipsalis
(Cactus/
Cactaceae
Family)

Characteristics: It's hard to recognize this genus as a cactus, since it's an epiphytic genus (non-parasitic plant that grows on other plants). The species of this genus grow on the surfaces of trees. It is also called "Reed cactus" and tends to be pendulous after it grows to a certain point. It has a variety of leaf types, some being flat, others being elongated and similar to stems. This plant likes filtered light and humid air and appreciates being sprayed with water.

Cultivation: These plants are relatively strong. Their growth is fast, and their stems are always growing. They can be grown in soft light as well, so it's safe to grow them indoors. Their flowers also bloom very easily from the tip of the stems. Since they like water, water often. In summer there's the potential for rot, so reduce the watering during those months.

Area of origin: Brazil

Ventilation ★★
Growth rate ★★

Rhipsalis cereuscula

Called "Coral cactus" for the shape of its branches, its stems are slim and grow gradually in a series of short shoots. During the growth season, new stems stretch and become long, growing new roots on their tips. Ultimately, the plant starts dangling because of its weight and keeps growing more and more roots. When it blooms transparent flowers, it uses them to self-pollinate and grow round seeds.

PART 3

Creating Succulent Arrangements

A miniature world

We matched the white design of the *Espostoa melanostele* with the stylish silver color of the aluminum. This makes the red and pink-colored succulents pop even more.

An enchanting ancient design

A garden setting with the small *Mammillaria bocasana* *'roseiflora'* growing its pink flower in the savanna. We planted different types of succulents along with it to achieve a natural-looking atmosphere.

Cacti in a rectangular vase

With the brown fluffy hair of the *Kalanchoe beharensis*
'Fang' and the white design of *Espostoa melanostele*, we
aim for a nice balance of brown, white and yellow colors.
We create a sense of unity ordering the cacti by height,
for a tidier look.

Observation through a magnifying glass

When looking at these plants through a magnifying glass, you can see a whole new world. There's a lot to see on a *Kalanchoe humilis*.

Round cacti in a round vase

We start by placing the largest cactus, the *Mammillaria candida var. rosea*, followed by *Mammillaria brauneana*. Then add a bit of an accent using *Kalanchoe humilis*. We finish the arrangement by adding some cacti with beautiful white spines, such as *Espostoa melanostele* and *Notocactus scopa*, and arranging them according to size and color.

A composition of green colors

We chose *Euphorbia trigona* as the main plant, because of its tall shape. With their future growth in mind, we also added *Euphorbia enopla ver.*, *Haworthia vittata* and *Crassula hirta*. To finish, we added the hanging *Crassula remota* in the foreground.

Family of Mesen

This composition is made of *Lithops, Conophytum* and *Fenestraria*. Since they are similar in nature, they get along well when planted near each other. This group of plants is called "Mesen" in Japanese, which means "female hermit." They are so called because of their smooth feminine skin.

A garden of succulents

We used *Adenia glauca* as our centerpiece and then planted some white cacti and succulents with thick leaves. The composition in the photo is one year old. It is well-established and its strong, beautiful form continues to evolve.

White planets

The shape and white color of *Epithelantha* are really the best. This composition is made exclusively of *Epithelantha micromeris*. Because of their slow growth, we grouped seedlings together in a small pot. We look forward to seeing how it will look when the flowers start blooming.

Tools and materials for planting and arranging

Arranging succulents is not that difficult and the required tools are not many. Ideally you want to use soil that gives good breathability and has water retention.

1 Small shovel

Use this to place soil when planting. Smaller ones are useful for smaller-sized plants.

2 Tweezers (large and small types)

These are used when planting seedlings, treating plants that have wrinkles and acclimating the soil. It's an essential part of the toolkit. Large tweezers are useful for dealing with larger-sized parts.

3 Spoon

This is useful to inserting into the soil when space is tight.

4 Scissors

For cutting roots and more.

5 Gloves

Leather gloves are useful when planting large cacti with sharp spines. When dealing with smaller cacti, using a pair of tweezers is often a better option.

6 Watering Can

Allows you to direct water where it's needed. It's okay to use alternatives like the pot you see here, or other spouted containers.

7 Soil for succulents

A blend of soil specifically used for cacti and succulents. It consists of small akadama soil mixed with charcoal and sand. This soil facilitates ventilation, drainage and water retention.

8 Akadama (medium grain)

When using a large container, place some of this soil along the bottom. It will help with breathability and drainage, thus helping prevent the root from rotting.

9 Pumice

A natural soil made of porous igneous rock. Its natural pattern is beautiful and it spruces up the look of your plantings. Because of its excellent water retention and drainage, it was originally used in the bottom of vases and bowls.

10 Sphagnum moss

Dried moss that can be used as a growing medium. It helps breathability and water retention, so it's used as soil for small arrangements.

11 Fertilizer

A chemical fertilizer, placed in small amounts at the bottom of the pots. Cacti should always be fertilized. Succulents, on the other hand, might get spoiled if too much fertilizer is applied, so use a very small amount.

12 Net

Used to cover the drainage hole in pots.

13 Newspaper pages

When placed in a pot with a drainage hole, the soil inside the pot will often be loose at first and will slip through the net for a while after replanting. Use newspaper to keep the area underneath the pot clean. Remove it after the soil has settled and the "shedding" has stopped.

Arranging your plants

Once you have found some succulents you like, why don't you challenge yourself and try to arrange your favorite plants? It's often easy to grow plants of the same genus or are similar in nature together.

Planting in soil

Use soil to grow succulent plants and cacti. The soil used has a base of akadama, which is great for breathability, drainage and water retention.

1 Prepare the pot.

2 Add soil until pot is about half full.

3 Try placing the plants inside to get an idea of the overall finished image.

4 Place your first plant and stabilize with soil.

5 Continue planting in the desired order.

6 When all the plants are arranged, cover their roots well with soil.

7 Give your pot a slight shake to let the soil settle firmly with the roots.

8 Done!

Planting in sphagnum moss

Sphagnum moss is a dried moss that is good for breathability and water retention, which makes it a good medium for small arrangements.

1 Place dry moss in a bowl and pour water over it.

2 Massage it well with fingers until it becomes mushy.

3 Prepare the pot.

4 When using a very small pot, add a small amount of fertilizer to the bottom.

5 Wrap the large seedlings in moss.

6 Place inside the pot.

7 Fill the pot with more moss and decide the position of your plants.

8 Plant smaller seedlings in the moss one by one.

9 Keep going until the end.

10 Done!

How to grow succulents

There are two ways to gradually grow new succulents from existing plants: leaf cutting and stem cutting.

Leaf cutting

Did you know there are plants that can naturally grow a new generation from just one leaf?

Succulents fall into this category. Propagating from leaves is possible because the leaves are thick and firm. If a leaf is dislodged from handling or from contact with an animal, it will grow a new plant in the spot where it lands. It's a distinctive breeding method, and very easy. We just reproduce the same process that happens in their normal life cycle. After removing a leaf, roll it gently on dried soil and leave it there (keep in mind which side is the upper one, as the plant will grow better if the leaf is planted with the upper side facing upwards). Leave the leaf without water until the sprouts or the roots start to emerge. When the leaf gets thin, and sprouts start to expand, start watering the leaf about once a week so it doesn't become too dry. What was originally the leaf will wither in order to nourish the new roots. Spring and fall are the proper times for this. The new offshoot will slowly grow into a cute miniature of the fully-grown adult plant. Please try this at home!

* Whether or not leaf cutting is possible depends on the species. It is usually possible in the case of succulents whose leaves come away easily from the stem.

Stem cutting (or Pruning)

Usually pruning is done for stems that are too long and are therefore disrupting the plant's balance. When the pruned upper part is put into soil, it starts growing new roots. This breeding method is called "stem cutting." We cut and place stems in dry soil and wait for them (without watering) to start growing new roots.

After growing the new roots, the planted stem becomes thin and gets wrinkly. At that point, we start watering. The proper seasons to do stem cutting are spring and fall. How long they take to grow new roots depends on the species and also depends on the place and time of replanting. Since it can vary so much, please observe the stem often and carefully.

If the part where the stem was cut is wide, leave it to dry for a few days before inserting the stem into soil.

Advice for growing succulents

Watering

Absolutely do not water daily. When the soil inside the pot is completely dry, water until the inner section of the soil becomes wet to a certain degree. It is important to moderate correctly the amount of water. The amount of water required is vastly affected by where the pot is placed, the soil and the plant species, so definitely take the time to research the needs of your particular plant. Succulents are more than 90 percent water and can be compared to water tanks. If their leaves start becoming thin, water them more often. By carefully observing your plant, you will get a feel for whether they want water or not.

Sunlight

Succulents love sunlight. If placed in environments similar to their area of origin, they grow even more beautifully, so always place them in well-lit environments.

If they don't receive enough sunlight:

1 The leaves open and spread and become thinner, trying to find light.
2 The size of leaves becomes gradually smaller.
3 The leaves become untidy and start to droop.

All of these are caused by the lack of sunlight. In fact, lack of sunlight is the most common reason that succulents wither and die. If your plants start showing mild symptoms, remember to move them to a well-lit spot in order to let them recover. If the symptoms are severe, do some pruning and let the stems grow again. Artificial lighting has no effect. They need to receive direct sunlight.

Seasonal advice

Spring: Growth season. Water often during this time. The leaves lose their bright colors and might get thinner; this is also part of their natural cycle so don't worry about it. It's easy for insects to be attracted to these plants during spring, so make sure to check frequently and remove the insects immediately. Plants' growth easily stops if they don't receive enough light, so don't forget to keep them in a well-lit spot.

Summer: It can be a very tough period for succulents that are vulnerable to humidity. Water moderately and keep the succulents in well-ventilated places to avoid rot. Take precautions if you're going to be away from home for an extended period. Keep your plants slightly in shade to avoid sunburn and let them rest calmly.

Fall: Growth season. Many species change their color during this season. The species that rested in summer immediately come back to life when they receive water. The leaves become thick and their colors vibrant. If left under enough sunlight during this season, the color of the plants will improve and will be nicer during winter too. Be aware that some species do not change color.

Winter: Most species will freeze and wither at temperatures under 32°F/ 0° C and are generally vulnerable to cold weather, so be sure to keep them in warm places and avoid watering. They do not grow during this season, but the beautiful fall leaves can still be enjoyed even in winter.

Glossary

Aerial root: Refers to roots grown outside of soil. There is a distinction between supporting roots and absorbing roots. Supporting roots help the body maintain its balance. Absorbing roots help absorb water.

Areole: Name of the part of cacti where spines grow. They are present on all the plants of the Cactaceae family.

Crawling: As the name suggests, some species grow crawling slowly on the ground.

Ecdysis/Skin shedding: In this phenomenon, the leaves form a round-shaped part which gradually spreads and from within this round shape a new leaf is formed. It occurs often in *Lithops* and *Conophytum* families.

Epiphyte species: These species grow plenty of roots outside the ground and attach to larger trees during their growth. They differ from parasitic species.

Fasciation/Cresting: Defines plant variations where the growth points have mutated into growth lines, usually causing stretched and unusual shapes. This phenomenon also causes the plants to grow in all directions. It is a rare mutation.

Flower bud: Name of the first stage of flower growth.

Flower stem: A name given to stems that stretch in search of sunlight in order to grow flowers.

Genus: Used to specify groups of plants that have similar structures or are similar in nature and can only be distinguished by subtle details. The genus is one step below Families and one step above Species. There are also subgenera (plural of subgenus) in some cases.

Genus name: The name that indicates a genus. They are usually either Latin or Latinized names and the first letter is always capitalized.

Growing en masse: Growing in clumps/clusters. Plants with this capacity repeatedly grow seedlings, causing this phenomenon where the plants grow as a group of single bodies.

Hair: Countless tissues grown on the body in order to protect it from cold and strong sunlight.

Leaf burning/Sunburn: Appears as discoloration on leaves when outer tissues are sun-damaged. This phenomenon happens to plants that are not used to sunlight. When suddenly placed under sunlight, the leaves can easily get sunburned. It can also be caused by strong sunlight in summer.

Leaf cutting: It's a method to grow stock where a single leaf is removed from the plant and replanted.

Lignification: In this phenomenon, the enlarged part of the stem turns hard in order to sustain the weight of the plant and also turns a brown color similar to wood. This phenomenon always starts from the roots.

Maculated/Spotted: A mutation that causes a species that in origin is completely green and monochromatic to grow a single part that has a yellow, white or red pattern instead.

Mimesis: Also known as camouflaging. Mimetic plants change their bodies to look similar to their environment, in order to protect themselves from animal damage.

Pruning: Activity in which longer parts are cut to adjust the shape and balance of the plant.

Pure breed: Ancestor species. They are in a state prior to improving in quality.

Rainforest type: Defines the species that grow in humid rainforests. They like humidity.

Root clogging: A state in which the roots have grown so much that they filled their own bowl and their growth has stopped.

Rosette: Name of the form when leaves spread a similarly to the petals of a rose flower, spreading in a radial shape.

Scientific name: The internationally accepted name used for plants. Usually the scientific names are a combination of the name of the genus and of the species, with the addition of variants.

Seed blowing: Phenomenon in which the seedlings fall directly from the parent plant.

Shade: A state in which light is being blocked in some way.

Stem cutting: A method of growing stock by which longer stems or branches are pruned and replanted.

Summer type species: Species that grow during summer. Most species fall under this category.

Tree-like species: Species that grow vertically in a tree shape.

White powder: A thin foundation-like powder that covers the leaves of many succulent species. It protects the leaves from strong sunlight.

Window: The slightly transparent part in the tip of Lens species' leaves that helps the plant absorb more light. It is a characteristic of the *Haworthia* and *Lithops* families.

Winter type species: Species that grow during winter. *Lithops*, *Conophytum* and *Crassula* families to name a few.

Index

Books to Span the East and West

Our core mission at Tuttle Publishing is to create books which bring people together one page at a time. Tuttle was founded in 1832 in the small New England town of Rutland, Vermont (USA). Our fundamental values remain as strong today as they were then—to publish best-in-class books informing the English-speaking world about the countries and peoples of Asia. The world is a smaller place today and Asia's economic, cultural and political influence has expanded, yet the need for meaningful dialogue and information about this diverse region has never been greater. Since 1948, Tuttle has been a leader in publishing books on the cultures, arts, cuisines, languages and literatures of Asia. Our authors and photographers have won many awards and Tuttle has published thousands of titles on subjects ranging from martial arts to paper crafts. We welcome you to explore the wealth of information available on Asia at **www.tuttlepublishing.com.**

Published by Tuttle Publishing, an imprint of Periplus Editions (HK) Ltd.

www.tuttlepublishing.com

ISBN 978-0-8048-5106-0

TANIKUSHOKUBUTSUZUKAN
Copyright © Misa Matsuyama 2012
English translation rights arranged with Nitto Shoin Honsha Co., Ltd. through Japan UNI Agency

Original Japanese edition:
Photography Shimomura Shinobu
Cover – Text design Hada Izumi
Revision Proofreading Corp. Kainoki
Editing Create ONO (Ohno Masayo)
Planning – Progress Kaburagi Kaori (Tatsumi Publishing Co., Ltd.)

English Translation ©2020 Periplus Editions (HK) Ltd.
Translated from Japanese by HL Language Services.

Library of Congress in Process

Distributed by:
North America, Latin America & Europe
Tuttle Publishing
364 Innovation Drive, North Clarendon
VT 05759-9436 U.S.A.
Tel: 1 (802) 773-8930; Fax: 1 (802) 773-6993
info@tuttlepublishing.com
www.tuttlepublishing.com

Japan
Tuttle Publishing
Yaekari Building 3rd Floor
5-4-12 Osaki Shinagawa-ku, Tokyo 141 0032
Tel: (81) 3 5437-0171; Fax: (81) 3 5437-0755
sales@tuttle.cop; wwwtuttleco.jp

Asia Pacific
Berkeley Books Pte. Ltd.
3 Kallag Sector, #04-01, Singapore 349278
Tel: (65) 67412178; Fax: (65) 67412179
inquiries@periplus.com.sg
www.tuttlepublishing.com

Printed in Malaysia   2008TO

23 22 21 20   10 9 8 7 6 5 4 3